The Roadmap to Small Business Growth

The art of scaling: 10 steps to grow a small business.

LYRA JAMES

Conducting request exploration to identify target guests.

Developing effective marketing strategies

using digital platforms for client accession

Chapter 6; erecting a High-Performing Team

Hiring the right gift for growth

Cultivating a positive work culture

Training and developing workers for scalability.

Chapter 7; Establishing Strategic Hookups.

relating implicit mates for collaboration

Securing backing for expansion

Chapter 10; Monitoring and Conforming to Continued Growth

enforcing performance tracking systems

Assaying data and making data-driven opinions

Continuously conforming strategies for sustainable growth

Note The chapter titles and contents are grounded on the general theme of spanning a small business. Feel free to modify or customize them according to your specific requirements and preferences.

Chapter 1

Preface to Spanning a Small Business

Spanning a small business is an instigative yet grueling bid that can lead to significant growth and success. In this chapter, we will claw into the concept of scaling, explore why it's pivotal for small business growth, and bandy the benefits and challenges associated with scaling.

Scaling refers to the process of growing a business in a sustainable and profitable manner. It involves expanding operations, adding profit, and reaching a larger client base while maintaining effectiveness and profitability. While every small business dreams of achieving substantial growth, scaling requires careful planning, strategic decision-timber, and effective prosecution.

One of the primary reasons why scaling is essential for small business growth is the eventuality of increased profitability. By spanning their operations, businesses can take advantage of husbandry of scale, reducing costs per unit and adding profit perimeters. With increased product volumes, businesses can negotiate better deals with suppliers, lower product costs, and optimize their distribution networks. This, in turn, allows them to offer competitive pricing to guests while maintaining healthy profit perimeters.

Also, spanning a small business opens doors to new openings and requests. By expanding their client base geographically or tapping into new target requests, businesses can diversify their profit aqueducts and reduce reliance on a single request member. This not only helps alleviate pitfalls but also allows businesses to explore untapped requests and influence arising trends.

Another pivotal benefit of scaling is the capability to attract top gifts. As a business grows, it gains visibility and credibility, making it more seductive to professionals. spanning frequently requires hiring fresh workers with different skill sets to handle increased workloads and liabilities. This affluence of gifts brings fresh perspectives, moxie, and invention to the business, fueling further growth and success.

Still, spanning a small business isn't without its challenges. One of the most significant challenges is maintaining the same position of quality and client satisfaction while growing fleetly. As operations expand, businesses must ensure that their products or services constantly meet client prospects. This may bear developing robust quality control processes, enforcing standardized procedures, and investing in training programs to maintain thickness across the board.

Also, scaling can strain a small business's coffers, including finances, structure, and mortal capital.

Acceptable backing is frequently a prerequisite for scaling, as businesses may need to invest in new outfits, technology, marketing, and gift accession. Without proper fiscal planning and access to capital, businesses may struggle to sustain growth or face cash inflow challenges.

Likewise, spanning a small business necessitates effective operation and leadership. As a business expands, leaders must delegate liabilities, empower workers, and establish effective communication channels. Without strong leadership and effective delegation, scaling can lead to chaos, overwhelmed workers, and a decline in overall productivity.

To overcome these challenges and successfully gauge a small business, entrepreneurs and business possessors need to develop a comprehensive scaling strategy. This strategy should encompass clear pretensions and objects, an analysis of the business's strengths and sins, a thorough understanding of the target request, and a roadmap for perpetration.

In conclusion, spanning a small business is a transformative trip that can lead to substantial growth and success. It offers increased profitability, access to new requests, and the occasion to attract top gifts. still, scaling also presents challenges related to maintaining quality, managing coffers, and sustaining effective leadership. Developing a well-allowed

 - By scaling strategy and addressing these challenges proactively, small businesses can unleash their full eventuality and achieve long-term growth and substance.

Chapter 2

Defining Your Business Goals and Vision

In the trip of spanning a small business, one of the critical ways is defining clear pretensions and establishing a compelling vision. This chapter will claw into the significance of setting business pretensions, the process of defining them, and the significance of casting a vision for your business's future.

Setting clear and specific pretensions is vital for several reasons. originally, pretensions give direction and purpose. They serve as a roadmap, guiding the conduct and opinions of the business towards an asked outgrowth. Without clear pretensions, a business can fluently get lost in the day-to-day operations and lose sight of its long-term objectives.

Secondly, pretensions serve as a standard for measuring progress and success. By setting specific targets and mileposts, a business can track its performance and estimate whether it is on track to achieving its objectives. This allows for regular assessment and adaptation of strategies to ensure nonstop enhancement and alignment with the overall vision.

To define effective business pretensions, it's important to follow a structured process. Begin by conducting a thorough assessment of your current business position. This includes assaying your strengths, sins, openings, and pitfalls (geek analysis). Identify the areas that bear enhancement, the openings to subsidize on, and the implicit challenges to overcome.

Next, set SMART pretensions Specific, Measurable, Attainable, Applicable, and Time-bound. Specific pretensions easily define what you want to achieve, similar to adding profit by a certain chance or expanding into a new request member. Measurable pretensions allow for quantifiable shadowing of progress, similar to acquiring a certain number of new guests within a specific timeframe. Attainable pretensions are realistic and attainable, considering the available coffers and capabilities of the business. Applicable pretensions align with the overall business objectives and contribute to the long-term vision. Incipiently, time-bound pretensions have a specific timeline or deadline for completion, furnishing a sense of urgency and responsibility.

It's also important to align your business pretensions with your bourns and values. As an entrepreneur or business proprietor, your pretensions and values should harmonize with the pretensions of your business. This alignment ensures that you are motivated, passionate, and committed to the pursuit of these objects, which is essential for long-term success.

In addition to setting pretensions, casting a vision for your business's future is inversely pivotal. A vision is a clear and inspiring picture of what you aspire your business to come. It provides a sense of direction, motivates workers, and attracts stakeholders who partake in your vision. A compelling vision creates a unifying purpose that guides the conduct and opinions of the entire association.

To produce an effective vision, it is essential to suppose long-term and consider the larger impact your business can make. Ask yourself questions similar to what values and principles will guide your business. What impact do you want to have on your guests, assiduity, or society? How do you fantasize about your business's position in the request and its part in the lives of its guests?

An important vision statement should be terse, memorable, and inspiring. It should easily communicate the purpose and values of your business, landing the substance of what you aim to achieve. By participating in this vision with your platoon and stakeholders, you produce a collaborative sense of purpose and inspire them to work towards the consummation of that vision.

Once you have defined your business pretensions and drafted your vision, it's pivotal to communicate and regularly readdress them. Partake your pretensions and vision with your platoon, icing that everyone is aligned and understands their part in achieving these objectives. Regularly review and assess your progress towards your pretensions, making adaptations and advances as demanded. Also, keep your vision at the van of your decision-making processes, icing that every strategic move is in alignment with your long-term bourses.

In conclusion, defining clear pretensions and casting a compelling vision is a pivotal step in spanning a small business. It provides direction, purpose, and a standard for measuring progress. By following a structured process and setting SMART pretensions, businesses can effectively define their objects. Also, an important vision statement creates a unifying purpose and inspires stakeholders to contribute towards the consummation of that vision. By regularly reconsidering and communicating these pretensions and visions, businesses can stay on track, motivate their brigades, and achieve long-term success.

Chapter 3

Erecting a Strong Foundation

When it comes to spanning a small business, erecting a strong foundation is consummated. This chapter explores the crucial aspects involved in establishing a solid root that sets the stage for sustainable growth and success. We'll claw into strengthening core business processes, optimizing operations for scalability, and streamlining workflows and systems.

Strengthening core business processes is the first step toward erecting a strong foundation. This involves completely assessing and enriching the abecedarian processes that drive your business's day-to-day operations. Start by establishing your processes to gain clarity and identify areas that need enhancement. This includes conditioning similar to force operation, deals, and marketing processes, client relationship operation, and fiscal operation.

As you validate your processes, look for openings to streamline and automate tasks. This not only increases effectiveness but also reduces the chances of crimes and inconsistencies. Identify backups and inefficiencies that hamper productivity and apply results to exclude or minimize them. By strengthening your core processes, you lay the root for scalability, icing that as your business grows, it can handle increased demands without compromising quality or effectiveness.

Optimizing operations for scalability is another pivotal aspect of erecting a strong foundation. This involves assessing your current structure, coffers, and capabilities to determine if they can support the anticipated growth. Consider factors similar to product capacity, technology systems, physical space, and mortal coffers.

Still, you may need to make strategic investments in areas similar to technology upgrades, and outfits, if your structure is not scalable. For illustration, upgrading your IT structure to support increased data storehouse and processing capabilities or investing in an advanced ministry that can handle advanced product volumes. By proactively optimizing your operations, you produce a solid frame that can accommodate growth without passing significant dislocations or backups.

Streamlining workflows and systems is another critical aspect of erecting a strong foundation. This involves assessing how information, tasks, and communication inflow within your association. Identify areas where homemade processes can be automated, similar to enforcing design operation software or exercising client relationship operation (CRM) systems to streamline deals and support processes.

enforcing standardized workflows and systems not only increases effectiveness but also ensures thickness and reduces the threat of crimes. This is particularly important as your business scales and further workers come on board. Streamlined workflows and systems enable workers to unite seamlessly, access information fluently, and work more efficiently. It also allows for better visibility and shadowing of crucial criteria, enabling data-driven decision- timber.

In addition to streamlining workflows, establishing effective communication channels is pivotal for a strong foundation. As your business grows, communication becomes more complex, involving multiple brigades, departments, or indeed remote locales. enforcing robust communication systems, similar to design operation tools, instant messaging platforms, or regular platoon meetings, fosters collaboration aligns brigades and ensures everyone is working towards common pretensions.

erecting a strong foundation also involves developing a culture of nonstop enhancement. Encourage workers to laboriously seek out openings for process optimization and invention. Apply feedback mechanisms, similar to suggestion boxes or regular hand checks, to gather perceptivity and ideas for enhancement. Fete and award workers who contribute to enhancing effectiveness and effectiveness. By fostering a culture of nonstop enhancement, you produce a terrain that adapts and evolves as your business scales.

likewise, investing in hand training and development is vital for erecting a strong foundation. Equip your workers with the chops and knowledge necessary to exceed in their places and acclimatize to changing demands. give ongoing training programs, mentorship openings, or access to external coffers. Developing your pool not only enhances productivity but also builds a sense of fidelity and commitment to the business.

Incipiently, establishing strong internal controls and threat operation systems is pivotal for a strong foundation. As your business scales, the pitfalls and challenges you face may increase. apply internal controls to guard against fraud, cover sensitive data, and ensure compliance with regulations. Develop threat operation strategies that identify and address implicit pitfalls to your business's stability and growth. By proactively managing pitfalls, you can minimize dislocations and make adaptability in the face of misgivings.

In conclusion, erecting a strong foundation is vital for spanning a small business. Strengthening core business processes, optimizing operations, streamlining workflows and systems, establishing effective communication channels, fostering a culture of nonstop enhancement, investing in hand training and development, and enforcing robust internal controls and threat operation systems are crucial rudiments in establishing solid roots for sustainable growth. By proactively fastening on these aspects, businesses can place themselves for success as they navigate the

Chapter 4

Developing a Scalable Business Model

In the hunt to gauge a small business, developing a scalable business model is pivotal. This chapter explores the complications of creating a business model that can support and sustain growth. We will claw into assessing your business model, relating scalability backups, and enforcing changes to achieve scalability.

To begin, it's essential to estimate your being business model and assess its scalability eventuality. A business model encompasses how your company creates, delivers, and captures value. dissect each element of your business model, including your target request, value proposition, profit aqueducts, and cost structure. Identify the rudiments that may pose challenges to scalability.

One common scalability tailback

is a heavy reliance on homemade labor or substantiated services. While these approaches may work well for a small operation, they can hamper growth when gauged. Consider ways to streamline and automate processes, reducing reliance on individual moxie and enabling replication of successful processes.

Another scalability tailback

may lie in the limitations of your current technology structure. Outdated or shy systems can hamper scalability by limiting productivity, effectiveness, and the capability to handle increased demand. Assess your technology needs and invest in scalable results that can accommodate growth, similar to pall-grounded platforms, client relationship operation (CRM) systems, or enterprise resource planning (ERP) software.

likewise, consider the scalability of your profit aqueducts. Some profit models, similar as one- time deals or customized results, may not advance themselves well to scaling. Explore openings to diversify your profit aqueducts and incorporate recreating profit models, similar to subscriptions, enrollments, or empowering agreements. These models can give further predictable and scalable profit over time.

Once you have linked scalability backups, it's time to apply changes to achieve scalability. One approach is to regularize your processes and immolations. By defining clear and replicable processes, you produce a foundation for scalability. Standardization reduces variations, enhances effectiveness, and allows for easier training and onboarding of new workers as your business grows.

Consider modularizing your products or services. Breaking them down into modular factors allows for inflexibility and customization while enabling brisk and more effective scaling. Modularity can also grease the development of reciprocal products or services that expand your request reach and induce fresh profit aqueducts.

also, embracing technology and digital results is vital for scalability. influence robotization tools to streamline repetitious tasks, optimize workflows, and ameliorate productivity. apply client relationship operation (CRM) systems to manage client relations, track deals, and identify growth openings. Embracing digital marketing channels and analytics allows for targeted marketing juggernauts, precise followership segmentation, and a better understanding of client preferences.

also, establishing strategic hookups can fuel scalability. uniting with other businesses that round your immolations can help expand your reach and client base. Look for openings to influence each other's strengths and coffers. Strategic hookups can unleash new requests, participated moxie, and access to new distribution channels, all of which contribute to scalability.

Another aspect to consider is scalability in terms of geographical expansion. Assess the feasibility of entering new requests and expanding your client base beyond your current geographic boundaries. Conduct request exploration, identify target regions, and develop request entry strategies that align with your scalability pretensions. Expanding geographically can open new growth openings and diversify your profit sources.

likewise, concentrate on erecting strong client connections and fostering client fidelity. Satisfied guests can come as brand lawyers, pertaining your business to others and contributing to organic growth. Apply client retention strategies similar to fidelity programs, substantiated gests, and excellent client service. By investing in client connections, you produce a strong foundation for scalability through reprising business and positive word-of-mouth.

Incipiently, continuously cover and dissect crucial performance pointers (KPIs) to track your progress towards scalability pretensions. Regularly review fiscal criteria, client accession and retention rates, deals performance, and functional effectiveness. These perceptivities allow you to identify areas that bear enhancement and make data-driven opinions to optimize scalability sweats.

In conclusion, developing a scalable business model is a vital step in spanning a small business. Assessing your business model, relating scalability backups, and enforcing changes to achieve scalability are essential rudiments of this process. By homogenizing processes, modularizing immolations, embracing technology, establishing strategic hookups, exploring geographical expansion, fastening client connections, and covering performance pointers, businesses can produce a foundation for sustainable growth. By developing a scalable business model, you place your business for long-term success in a fleetly evolving business. path to scalability.

Chapter 5

Expanding Your Client Base

Expanding your client base is a pivotal step in spanning a small business. In this chapter, we will explore the strategies and tactics that can help you reach new guests and grow your business. We'll bandy the significance of request exploration, developing effective marketing strategies, and using digital platforms for client accession.

The first step in expanding your client base is conducting thorough request exploration. Understanding your target request is essential for relating implicit guests and acclimatizing your immolations to meet their requirements. Start by assaying demographic data, similar to age, gender, position, and income situations, to identify specific parts that align with your products or services.

Beyond demographics, claw into psychographic information to gain perceptivity into your target guests' preferences, interests, and values. This information can help you craft marketing dispatches that reverberate with your followership and separate your business from challengers.

Request exploration also involves assessing your challenges. Identify who your challengers are, what they offer, and how they place themselves in the request. dissect their strengths and sins to identify gaps or openings that you can subsidize on. By understanding your challengers, you can develop strategies that set your business piecemeal and attract guests.

Once you have a clear understanding of your target request, it's time to develop effective marketing strategies. Start by defining your unique selling proposition (USP), which highlights the unique benefits or advantages that your products or services offer. Your USP should reverberate with your target guests and separate you from challengers.

Craft compelling marketing dispatches that communicate your USP effectively. These dispatches should address the pain points or solicitations of your target followership and punctuate the value they will admit by choosing your business. Use conclusive language, liar ways, and emotional prayers to capture the attention and interest of implicit guests.

use colorful marketing channels to reach your target followership. Traditional marketing channels similar to print advertisements, direct correspondence, and original events can be effective for targeting specific geographic locales or demographics. still, digital marketing channels offer unequaled reach and targeting capabilities.

influence the power of digital platforms to expand your client base. Develop a strong online presence by creating a stoner-friendly and visually appealing website that showcases your products or services. Optimize your website for hunt machines (SEO) to ameliorate visibility and organic business. apply a content marketing strategy to give precious information to your target followership and place your business as an assiduity authority.

Social media platforms give you an occasion to engage with your target guests directly. Identify the platforms that your followership frequents and develop a presence there. produce engaging content, share in exchanges, and respond to client inquiries or feedback. Social media advertising allows for precise targeting, enabling you to reach specific demographics, interests, or actions.

In addition to social media, consider exercising dispatch marketing to nurture leads and make long-term connections with guests. Collect dispatch addresses through website sign-ups, elevations, or events, and produce substantiated dispatch juggernauts that deliver applicable content and offers to your subscribers.

unite with influencers or assiduity experts who have a significant following in your target request. Collaborating with influencers can help increase brand mindfulness and reach new guests who trust the recommendations of these influential individuals. Seek influencers whose values align with your brand and whose followership matches your target client profile.

Referral programs can also be an effective way to expand your client base. Encourage satisfied guests to relate your business to their musketeers, family, or associates by offering impulses or prices. apply a referral shadowing system to measure the success of your program and ensure that referrers are meetly honored.

likewise, consider expanding your client base geographically. However, explore openings to expand into new geographic areas, If your business operates in an original or indigenous request. Conduct request exploration to assess the demand and competition in those regions. Develop localized marketing strategies that reverberate with the specific requirements and preferences of guests in those areas.

Incipiently, track and dissect crucial criteria to estimate the success of your client expansion sweats. Examiner client accession costs, conversion rates, client continuance value, and other applicable KPIs to assess the effectiveness of your marketing strategies. Use this data to upgrade your approach and optimize your client accession sweats over time.

In conclusion, expanding your client base is a critical element of spanning a small business. By conducting request exploration, developing effective marketing strategies, and using digital platforms, you can reach new guests and grow your business. conform your marketing dispatches to reverberate with your target followership, use colorful marketing channels, and consider geographic expansion if applicable. Continuously track and dissect criteria to upgrade your approach and optimize your client accession sweats. By expanding your client base strategically, you place your business for sustainable growth and success.

Chapter 6

erecting a High-Performing Team

 Erecting a high-performing platoon is a critical factor in spanning a small business successfully. In this chapter, we will explore the significance of hiring the right gift, cultivating a positive work culture, and training and developing workers to support growth and achieve scalability.

 Hiring the right gift is the first step toward erecting a high-performing platoon. As your business scales, it's pivotal to attract individualities with the chops, moxie, and mindset that align with your association's values and pretensions. Take a strategic approach to reclamation by easily defining the places and liabilities, and the qualifications and rates you seek in campaigners.

Develop a comprehensive reclamation process that includes multiple stages similar to capsule webbing, interviews, chops assessments, and reference checks. Consider incorporating behavioral or situational interviews to assess how campaigners respond to real-life scripts and demonstrate problem-working and critical thinking chops.

Look for individuals who not only retain the necessary specialized chops but also parade rates similar to rigidity, collaboration, and a growth mindset. Seek out campaigners who show a genuine interest in your assiduity and a passion for literacy and development.

Cultivating a positive work culture is vital for erecting a high-performing platoon. A positive work culture fosters hand engagement, collaboration, and commitment to the association's pretensions. Start by defining your company's core values and icing they're integrated into every aspect of your business. Communicate these values to workers and support them through conduct and actions.

produce an inclusive and probative work terrain where workers feel valued, admired, and empowered. Encourage open communication, collaboration, and the exchange of ideas. Establish clear channels for feedback and encourage workers to partake in their studies, enterprises, and suggestions for enhancement.

Fete and award hand achievements and benefactions. apply performance evaluation systems that give formative feedback and identify areas for growth. give openings for professional development and career advancement to keep workers engaged and motivated.

Invest in hand training and development to enhance their chops and capabilities. Offer both formal and informal training programs that align with your business pretensions and individual hand development plans. give openings for cross-functional training, mentorship, and knowledge sharing to encourage nonstop literacy and growth.

Empower workers by delegating responsibility and granting them autonomy in their places. Give them the freedom to make opinions and take the power of their work. Encourage invention and creativity by creating a terrain that welcomes new ideas and embraces calculated pitfalls.

Effective communication is a foundation of a high-performing platoon. Establish clear communication channels that promote translucency and foster collaboration. Conduct regular platoon meetings to keep everyone informed about the business's progress, pretensions, and challenges. Encourage active listening and open dialogue and give openings for workers to contribute their perspectives and ideas.

Leadership plays a vital part in erecting a high-performing platoon. Effective leaders inspire and motivate workers, give guidance and support, and lead by illustration. They produce a participating vision and give clarity on prospects, pretensions, and strategies. Effective leaders empower their platoon members, trust their moxie, and encourage them to take power and action.

Delegate tasks and liabilities grounded on individualities' strengths and interests. give ongoing feedback and coaching to help workers develop their chops and reach their full eventuality. Encourage nonstop growth and enhancement by setting challenging yet attainable pretensions and furnishing the necessary coffers and support to meet them.

erecting a high-performing platoon also involves fostering a culture of collaboration and cooperation. Encourage cross-functional collaboration and produce openings for workers from different departments or brigades to work together on systems or enterprises. Promote a sense of concinnity and participated purpose that transcends individual places and promotes collaboration towards common pretensions.

In conclusion, erecting a high-performing platoon is pivotal for spanning a small business successfully. Hiring the right gift, cultivating a positive work culture, and investing in hand training and development are crucial rudiments of this process. Establish clear communication channels, empower workers, and give leadership that inspires and motivates. Foster collaboration and cooperation to influence the collaborative chops and moxie of your platoon members. By erecting a high-performing platoon, you produce a strong foundation for spanning your business and achieving long-term success.

Chapter 7

Establishing Strategic hookups

Establishing strategic hookups is a vital step in spanning a small business. In this chapter, we will explore the significance of relating implicit mates, negotiating palm-palm alliances, and using coffers and moxie through strategic collaborations.

Strategic hookups can give multitudinous benefits to small businesses. They offer openings to pierce new requests, expand client reach, valve into reciprocal coffers, and enhance competitiveness. By joining forces with strategic mates, businesses can work on each other's strengths, alleviate sins, and achieve collective growth and success.

The first step in establishing strategic hookups is to identify implicit mates that align with your business objectives. Look for businesses that partake analogous values, target analogous client parts, or offer reciprocal products or services. Research your assiduity and explore networking events, trade shows, and online platforms to identify implicit mates.

Consider the strategic fit between your business and implicit mates. estimate how cooperation can help you achieve your scalability pretensions and how you can contribute to the growth of your mate. Assess their moxie, character, and request presence. Look for mates who bring unique coffers, capabilities, or distribution channels that can enhance your business's competitive advantage.

Once you have linked implicit mates, it is important to approach them with a palm-palm mindset. Develop a compelling value proposition that highlights the benefits and openings that cooperation can bring to both parties. Demonstrate how collaboration can produce value, increase profit, reduce costs, or enhance client satisfaction.

Initiate exchanges with implicit mates to explore participated pretensions, collective interests, and areas of collaboration. Be set to articulate your business's unique strengths and the value you bring to cooperation. At the same time, listen laboriously to understand the requirements, challenges, and pretensions of your implicit mates.

Negotiating mutually salutary cooperation requires effective communication and collaboration. easily define the places, liabilities, and prospects of each party. Establish crucial performance pointers (KPIs) to measure the success of the cooperation. bandy how coffers, pitfalls, and prices will participate participated, and develop a formal agreement that outlines the terms and conditions of the cooperation.

Collaboration and communication are essential throughout the cooperation. Regularly assess the progress of the cooperation and acclimate strategies as demanded. Maintain open lines of communication, address any issues or conflicts instantly, and celebrate participated successes. Translucency, trust, and effective communication form the foundation for successful strategic cooperation.

Strategic hookups can take colorful forms depending on the nature of the collaboration. Some common types of hookups include common gambles, empowering agreements, distribution hookups, andro-marketing juggernauts. Choose the type of cooperation that aligns with your business pretensions and provides the most value for both parties.

A common adventure involves combining coffers and moxie to pursue a specific design or occasion. This type of cooperation allows businesses to partake in pitfalls, costs, and prices, and influence each other's strengths to achieve a common ideal. common gambles can be particularly salutary when entering new requests or developing new products or services.

Licensing agreements enable businesses to work on their intellectual property (IP) by granting rights to another party in exchange for royalties or licensing freight. This type of cooperation allows businesses to expand their reach and induce profit using their IP by other companies.

Distribution hookups involve uniting with other businesses to distribute and vend products or services. This allows businesses to tap into distribution channels and gain access to new client parts. Distribution hookups can be particularly salutary for businesses looking to enter new requests or expand their request reach.

Co-marketing juggernauts involve uniting with another business to promote products or services through a common marketing enterprise. By pooling coffers, businesses can reach a larger followership, increase brand mindfulness, and share marketing costs. Co-marketing juggernauts can be particularly effective in targeting specific client parts or addressing a participated client need.

In addition to external hookups, businesses can also explore internal collaborations within their association. Encourage cross-functional collaboration and cooperation to influence the different chops and moxie of your workers. Foster a culture that promotes knowledge sharing, idea generation, and collaboration across departments.

Likewise, businesses can explore hookups with academic institutions, exploration associations, or assiduity associations. These hookups can give access to exploration and development coffers, specialized moxie, or assiduity perceptivity that can drive invention and competitiveness.

In conclusion, establishing strategic hookups is a precious strategy for spanning a small business. By relating implicit mates, negotiating palm-palm alliances, and using coffers and moxie, businesses can unleash new openings, expand their client base, and enhance competitiveness. Approach hookups with a cooperative mindset and develop a clear value proposition. Maintain open communication, translucency, and trust throughout the cooperation. Choose the type of cooperation that aligns with your pretensions and provides the most value for both parties. By erecting strong strategic hookups, businesses can accelerate their growth and achieve long-term success.

Chapter 8
Embracing Technology and Innovation

In the moment's fleetingly evolving business geography, embracing technology and invention is essential for spanning a small business. This chapter explores the significance of using technology results, enforcing robotization and digital tools, and staying streamlined with assiduity trends and inventions.

Embracing technology offers multitudinous benefits for small businesses. It enhances functional effectiveness, improves productivity, enables better decision- timber, and provides a competitive edge.

Technology can streamline processes, automate repetitious tasks, and free up precious time and coffers for strategic enterprise and growth-concentrated conditioning.

One key aspect of embracing technology is relating to the right results for your business. Start by assessing your current operations and areas that can profit from technological advancements. For illustration, consider espousing client relationship operation (CRM) software to manage and nurture client connections effectively. apply design operation tools to streamline workflows, ameliorate collaboration, and ensure timely design delivery. Explore force operation systems to optimize stock situations, reduce costs, and ameliorate force chain effectiveness.

pall computing is another precious technology to consider. Pall-grounded results offer scalability, inflexibility, and cost savings by allowing businesses to pierce software, storehouse, and calculate power through the internet. pall computing enables remote work, data backup and recovery, and easy scalability as your business grows.

Robotization is an important tool that can revise business processes and drive scalability. Estimate your operations to identify tasks that can be automated, similar to data entry, force operation, or client support. Enforcing robotization not only improves effectiveness but also reduces crimes, enhances thickness, and allows your platoon to concentrate on high-value conditioning.

Digital tools play a pivotal part in spanning a small business. Invest in tools that streamline communication, collaboration, and design operation. videotape conferencing platforms enable remote meetings and foster collaboration among geographically dispersed brigades. Collaboration tools like design operation software or participated document platforms allow for effective collaboration and document sharing.

Digital marketing tools are also essential for expanding your reach and attracting new guests. Dispatch marketing platforms enable targeted juggernauts and substantiated communication. Social media operation tools grease scheduling, monitoring, and assaying social media conditioning. Website analytics tools give perceptivity into website business, the caller gets.

, and conversion rates.

Staying streamlined with assiduity trends and inventions is pivotal for maintaining a competitive edge. Technology and diligence evolve fleetly, and businesses need to keep pace with the most advanced advancements. Stay connected with assiduity news, share in conferences and forums, and engage with assiduity experts and allowed.

leaders.

also, encourage a culture of invention within your association. Foster a terrain that welcomes creativity, trial, and the generation of new ideas. Encourage workers to explore innovative results, challenge processes, and contribute to the nonstop enhancement of the business. Apply mechanisms for idea sharing and collaboration, similar to brainstorming sessions, invention challenges, or suggestion programs.

Consider establishing hookups or collaborations with technology companies or startups. Uniting with innovative associations can give access to slice-edge technologies, moxie, and fresh perspectives. These hookups can fuel invention and give openings force-creation of new products or services.

 Likewise, keep an eye on rising technologies that have the eventuality to disrupt your assiduity. Technologies similar to artificial intelligence (AI), machine literacy, blockchain, and the Internet of Effects (IoT) are transubstantiating colorful sectors. estimate how these technologies can be applied to your business to drive invention, ameliorate client guests, or enhance functional effectiveness.

 It's pivotal to prioritize cybersecurity when embracing technology. With increased reliance on digital tools and platforms, businesses must guard their data and cover client information. apply robust cybersecurity measures, similar to encryption, multi-factor authentication, and regular data backups. Educate workers on cybersecurity stylish practices and establish protocols for data protection and incident response.

Training and upskilling workers in technology operations and digital chops are essential. ensure that your platoon has the necessary knowledge and capabilities to influence technology effectively. Offer training programs, shops, or access to online courses to enhance their digital knowledge. Encourage nonstop literacy and produce openings for workers to stay streamlined with the most technological advancements.

In conclusion, embracing technology and invention is a crucial motorist of scalability for small businesses. By using technology results, enforcing robotization and digital tools, and staying streamlined with assiduity trends, businesses can ameliorate effectiveness, drive invention, and gain a competitive advantage. Identify the right technology results for your business, automate processes, and invest in digital tools that streamline communication and collaboration. Stay connected with assiduity trends, foster a culture of invention, and consider hookups with technology companies. Prioritize cybersecurity and invest in hand training to ensure effective technology relinquishment. By embracing technology and invention, businesses can place themselves for growth and success in the digital age.

Chapter 9
Managing Finances for Growth

Managing finances effectively is a pivotal aspect of spanning a small business. In this chapter, we will explore the significance of fiscal planning, optimizing cash inflow, penetrating backing options, and covering crucial fiscal criteria to support business growth.

Fiscal planning is an abecedarian step in managing finances for growth. It involves creating a comprehensive roadmap that outlines the fiscal pretensions and strategies of your business. Start by setting realistic fiscal targets and creating a budget that aligns with your growth objectives. Break down your budget into different orders similar to deals and marketing, operations, exploration and development, and gift accession.

Regularly review and modernize your fiscal plan to reflect changes in your business geography and pretensions. Consider implicit pitfalls and misgivings and develop contingency plans to alleviate them. A well-defined fiscal plan provides a clear direction for managing coffers and making strategic fiscal opinions.

Optimizing cash inflow is pivotal for sustaining growth and icing the smooth operation of your business. Cash inflow operation involves covering the flux and exodus of cash to maintain acceptable working capital. Delayed payments from guests or inordinate force can tie up precious cash while managing accounts outstanding and negotiating favorable payment terms can ameliorate cash inflow.

utensil effective invoicing and collection processes to minimize payment detainments. Offer impulses for early payment or consider using technology results that streamline billing and payment processes. Regularly review your account's delinquency and follow up on outstanding checks to ensure timely payment.

Managing charges is another important aspect of cash inflow optimization. Continuously estimate your charges and identify areas where you can reduce costs without compromising the quality of your products or services. Negotiate with merchandisers for better pricing or explore indispensable suppliers. Consider enforcing cost-saving measures similar to energy-effective practices or exercising pall-grounded software to reduce structure costs.

penetrating backing options is frequently necessary for supporting growth enterprise. estimate different backing sources to determine the stylish fit for your business. Traditional options include bank loans, lines of credit, or small business subventions. Explore government programs or impulses that may be available for businesses in your assiduity or region.

In addition, indispensable backing sources similar to angel investors, adventure plutocrats, or crowdfunding platforms can give access to capital and moxie. When seeking backing, easily articulate your growth plans, demonstrate the implicit return on investment, and present a solid business case to implicit investors or lenders.

Maintaining accurate and over-to-date fiscal records is pivotal for effective fiscal operation. apply robust account systems and practices to track income, charges, and cash inflow. Regularly attune bank statements and cover fiscal deals to identify any disagreements or irregularities.

Monitoring crucial fiscal criteria allows you to assess the health and performance of your business. These criteria may include profit growth rate, gross profit periphery, net profit periphery, and return on investment. assaying these criteria enables you to identify trends, estimate the effectiveness of your strategies, and make informed fiscal opinions.

The cash conversion cycle is another critical metric to cover. It measures the time it takes for cash to inflow in and out of your business. By reducing the cash conversion cycle, you can optimize cash inflow and ameliorate working capital operations.

Likewise, assaying fiscal rates similar to liquidity rates, profitability rates, and influence rates provides perceptivity into the fiscal stability and effectiveness of your business. Compare these rates against assiduity marks or literal data to identify areas that bear enhancement or to punctuate your strengths.

Consider working with fiscal professionals similar to accountants or fiscal counsels to insure accurate fiscal reporting and gain expert perceptivity in managing your finances. They can give guidance on duty planning, fiscal soothsaying, and threat operation strategies.

Regularly review and modernize your fiscal plan, conforming strategies as demanded. Conduct periodic fiscal checkups to assess the delicacy and compliance of your fiscal records. This helps identify any areas of concern and ensures that your business remains financially healthy and biddable with legal and nonsupervisory conditions.

In conclusion, managing finances effectively is pivotal for spanning a small business successfully. fiscal planning, optimizing cash inflow, penetrating backing options, and covering crucial fiscal criteria are essential factors of fiscal operation for growth. Develop a comprehensive fiscal plan, optimize cash inflow through effective invoicing and expenditure operation, and explore backing options that align with your growth objectives. Maintain accurate fiscal records, cover crucial fiscal criteria, and seek professional advice when necessary. By effectively managing finances, businesses can support the growth of enterprises and ensure long-term fiscal stability.

Chapter 10

Monitoring and confirming for Continued Growth

Monitoring and conforming to changes in the business terrain is pivotal for sustained growth. In this final chapter, we will explore the significance of covering crucial performance pointers (KPIs), conducting regular performance evaluations, embracing a culture of nonstop enhancement, and being nimble in responding to request dynamics.

Monitoring crucial performance pointers (KPIs) is essential for tracking the progress and success of your business's growth enterprise.

KPIs are quantifiable criteria that reflect the performance and effectiveness of colorful aspects of your business. They give precious perceptivity into areas similar as deals, marketing, operations, client satisfaction, and fiscal performance.

Identify the KPIs that are most applicable to your business pretensions and track them constantly. This may include criteria similar to profit growth rate, client accession costs, client retention rate, conversion rates, or profitability rates. Dissect these KPIs regularly to estimate performance trends, identify areas for enhancement, and make data-driven opinions.

Regular performance evaluations are pivotal for assessing the effectiveness of your strategies and relating areas for enhancement. Conduct performance evaluations at destined intervals, similar to daily or annually, to review progress and give feedback to workers and brigades. Assess the achievement of pretensions, alignment with the business's vision, and the overall impact of enforced strategies.

During performance evaluations, encourage open and honest communication. give formative feedback, admit achievements, and address areas that need enhancement. Use this occasion to align individual pretensions with the business's objects and identify development openings to enhance hand chops and capabilities.

Embrace a culture of nonstop enhancement within your association. Encourage workers to seek out innovative results, challenge the status quo, and contribute ideas for process optimization and improvement. Apply feedback mechanisms similar to suggestion boxes, regular platoon meetings, or hand checks to gather perceptivity and perspectives.

Regularly review your business processes, workflows, and strategies to identify areas that can be meliorated or optimized. Consider the relinquishment of new technologies, the perpetration of assiduity stylish practices, or the reengineering of processes to enhance effectiveness and effectiveness. Non-stop enhancement is a mindset that fosters invention and enables businesses to acclimatize to changing request conditions and client prospects.

Be nimble and responsive to request dynamics and client feedback. Examiner assiduity trends, contender conditioning, and changes in client preferences. Stay connected with your target request through client checks, feedback forms, or social media engagement. Gather perceptivity to understand evolving client requirements and acclimatize your products, services, or marketing strategies consequently.

Embrace technology results that enable inflexibility and dexterity. Pal-grounded systems, design operation tools, and collaboration platforms grease flawless communication, remote work, and rapid-fire decision-timber. influence these technologies to respond snappily to request changes, client demands, or unlooked-for challenges.

Stay informed about assiduity trends and arising technologies that have the eventuality to disrupt your business. Attend conferences, assiduity events, or webinars to expand your knowledge and network with experts in your field. Engage with assiduity associations, allowed.

leaders, or instructors to gain perceptivity and stay streamlined with the rearmost developments.

Regularly readdress your business plan and assess its applicability and effectiveness in the current request geography. Consider external factors similar to changes in regulations, profitable conditions, or technological advancements. Review and modernize your strategies and pretensions to ensure they remain aligned with your business's vision and the evolving request dynamics.

Incorporate threat operation strategies into your monitoring and adaptation processes. Identify implicit pitfalls that could impact your business's growth and develop contingency plans to alleviate them. Regularly assess the effectiveness of your threat operation measures and acclimate them as necessary.

Eventually, foster a culture of collaboration and literacy within your association. encourage cross-functional collaboration, knowledge sharing, and platoon community. grease openings for workers to enhance their chops and stay streamlined with assiduity trends through training programs, shops, or access to external coffers.

In conclusion, monitoring and conforming for uninterrupted growth is pivotal for the long-term success of a small business. Examiner crucial performance pointers to track progress and make data-driven opinions. Conduct regular performance evaluations and embrace a culture of nonstop enhancement. Stay nimble and responsive to request dynamics and client feedback. Embrace technology results that enable inflexibility and dexterity. Stay informed about assiduity trends and arising technologies. Readdress and modernize your business plan to remain aligned with the evolving request geography. Incorporate threat operation strategies and foster a culture of collaboration and literacy. By laboriously covering and conforming, businesses can sustain growth and thrive in a dynamic business terrain.

Spanning a small business requires a delicate balance of strategic planning, invention, and rigidity. This comprehensive companion presents ten pivotal ways to help entrepreneurs and small business possessors navigate the art of spanning successfully. By enforcing these crucial strategies, businesses can witness substantial growth and take their gambles to new heights.

Define Your Vision and pretensions

Launch by clarifying your long-term vision for the business. Set specific, measurable, attainable, applicable, and time-bound (SMART) pretensions that align with your vision. Easily understanding your objects will give a solid foundation for the scaling process.

Conduct a Thorough Market Analysis

Conduct a comprehensive request analysis to identify openings and implicit challenges. Understand your target followership, challengers, and assiduity trends. This information will enable you to knit your growth strategy effectively.

Strengthen Your Core Operations

Before scaling, ensure that your core operations are optimized and effective. Streamline processes, identify backups, and apply systems to handle increased demand. A strong foundation will help functional issues from hindering growth.

Focus on client Experience

Client satisfaction is essential for sustainable growth. Prioritize client experience by laboriously seeking feedback, responding to queries, and furnishing exceptional service. Pious guests can come important lawyers for your brand.

Make a Strong platoon

As your business expands, you will need a competent and motivated platoon to support growth. Hire individuals who align with your company's values and retain the chops demanded to drive success. Foster a positive work culture to retain top gifts.

Develop a Marketing Strategy

Craft a well-defined marketing strategy to reach a broader followership. Use digital marketing, content creation, social media, and other channels to raise brand mindfulness and attract implicit guests.

Explore New Deals Channels

Diversify your deals channels to increase profit aqueducts. Consider expanding into online commerce, collaborating with resellers, or exploring B2B openings. Embrace invention to stay ahead of the competition.

Invest in Technology

Influence technology to automate tasks, enhance productivity, and gather precious data perceptivity. Use client relationship operation (CRM) software to ameliorate client relations and make data-driven opinions.

Monitor Financial Performance

Maintain a clear view of your fiscal performance and track crucial performance pointers (KPIs). Regularly review budgets, cash inflow, and profit perimeters to ensure you stay on track toward your scaling pretensions.

Acclimatize and Evolve

Inflexibility is pivotal in the scaling process. Continuously estimate your strategies and acclimate them grounded on request changes and client feedback. Embrace invention and be willing to pivot when necessary.

Conclusion

Spanning a small business requires fidelity, strategic planning, and a commitment to nonstop enhancement. By following the ten ways outlined in this companion, entrepreneurs, and small business possessors can confidently navigate the art of scaling and achieve sustainable growth. Flashback that scaling is not a one-time event but an ongoing process that requires rigidity and a client-centric approach. With a clear vision, a strong platoon, and a well-executed strategy, small businesses can place themselves for

long- term success and stand out in
their separate diligence

2

What Readers Are Saying

"Even the most intense drama benefits from dabs of humor, and Dunn's easy-to-follow formulas can help anyone add that crucial element to their novel."

Susan Miura
Author, *Show Me a Sign* (Young Adult Fiction)

"Upon reading *Making Fiction Funny! How To Create Story Humor*, I was blown away by the author's detailed knowledge of not only how to recognize comedy, but also how to construct it within a story. Most people (myself very much included) look at humor as a reactionary, visceral response, but Dunn takes it one step further and discusses tips and tricks for the reader to implement in order to create gut-busting scenes within their work.

As a Creative Writing Instructor, I plan to use Dunn's book in upcoming courses about incorporating humor into my students' stories. And as an author myself, I found the different examples and definitions of comedy extremely beneficial, and the correlating writing ideas/exercises within each section helped to bring a hands on element to the subject matter. Whether you're a comedy writer or not, do yourself a favor and buy this book!"

Dave Burns
Author, *A Million Little Gods: The Clearwater Chronicles*
Founder, The Ottawa Writers' Guild

"I write fiction and had been searching for a way to add humor to my stories. I bought at least four other books before I found this one. This is the best one for authors. The writer gives examples of what makes readers laugh. The information is easy to digest and makes sense to the average guy."